DAVID HARSENT

*

Mister Punch

Oxford   New York
OXFORD UNIVERSITY PRESS
1984

Oxford University Press, Walton Street, Oxford OX2 6DP
London New York Toronto
Delhi Bombay Calcutta Madras Karachi
Kuala Lumpur Singapore Hong Kong Tokyo
Nairobi Dar es Salaam Cape Town
Melbourne Auckland
and associated companies in
Beirut Berlin Ibadan Mexico City Nicosia

Oxford is a trade mark of Oxford University Press

British Library Cataloguing in Publication Data

Harsent, David
Mister Punch.
I. Title
821'.914   PR6058.A6948
ISBN 0-19-211966-4

Set by Getset (Bowden Typesetting Services) Limited
Printed in Great Britain by
J. W. Arrowsmith Ltd
Bristol

To Jane

Acknowledgements

Two of these poems appeared in my last collection, *Dreams of the Dead* (OUP, 1977). Others have appeared in the following publications: *Bananas, Encounter*, the *Poetry Review*, Poetry Book Society Supplements for Winter 1981, Winter 1982, Winter 1983, the *New Statesman*, the *London Magazine*, the *Literary Review*, and on Radio 3's *Poetry Now*.

Contents

. . . the wounded wounder is the agent of healing . . .
C. G. Jung

Mr Punch

The tiercel feathers upwind
breasting the airstream;
there's game on the slopes.

Guests on the valley floor
spread their picnic cloths—
midgets warped by the mid-day haze.

In the tangle of brush near the pines
unseen animals go belly-down,
hot beneath their tawny pelts.

White linen on the furze,
ribbons and flags,
skyline clouds a belladonna blue.—

The stasis breaks. A child
is tapping a wineglass on his teeth.
His friends join hands to dance

as lust explodes in the bracken.
Mr Punch worms into the girl
and she squeals like a peccary.

Over his shoulder, she glimpses
the hunting bird
plumbing an acre of sky

while her blood heats.
Mr Punch is growling; the breeze
cools the sweat on his flanks.

His wife and family feast
and watch the dancers.
These women are all alike to Mr Punch.

He'd like to own them, he'd like to eat them whole,
he'd like their murders
feeding his night-time conscience.

This one's something special:
she loves a dare
and Punchinello thrives on secrecy.

Suddenly, horses are there on the hillside,
standing by their shadows to feed.
Distant, they seem to be

behind a wall of glass.
They peel off, circling the dark patches of clover.
A dozen faces look up

struck through with happiness.
White light flashes from silverware,
the wineglass sings

along its breaking-line.
Mr Punch emerges, grinning.
The children dance in their ring.

Punch on Location

Hill country in rainy weather,
all other sounds subdued
by the hoarseness of water in the throat of the valley,

until the sky silvers and light swills the grass
like the glow in a green bowl.
Some women are bunched

by a fringe of dripping trees at the valley's lip,
packed like a herd,
their children mute and clinging: as it was

before the fruity heat of kitchens, before
the symmetry of gardens, the stealth
of embroidery, before marriage.

He sees the great canvasses animate at last,
Diana grazed by lust,
the Bacchae yelling and feeding off flesh . . .

His field-glasses catch blood on a chin,
the long, hard muscle in a naked thigh
flexing and bunching,

dark caps of hair
barbered with a knife and oiled.
They find the best in nature, stay alive

through everything, sleep when they can.
They're Punch's flock. He wrote the script for this.
He brings the cameras on.

Punch's Pathetic Fallacy

The sea a toneless abstract of the sea . . .
shingle, tideline, the void.

He spread his coat
on the cliff's pinnacle. A kestrel
was circling below him;
gulls were circling above. He heard
the tin ring of timber at the saw.

Alone, he shrank
to a shuttered eye. The kestrel came
from behind his head like a jet
to smash
something on the cliff-path.
It screamed and rose.

He leaped to his feet. His companion
(who was she?) leaped
with her hands at her throat.

'It was wonderful.' He ground his teeth. 'It was
wonderful, wonderful, wonderful.'
She sat down,
back to the wind, to tackle
a braid the wind had unpicked,
plain on her face
pique at his boyishness.

It wasn't like that (was it?)
but he enjoyed
the sensation of shrinking
and wept for how lovely the gulls were.

He descended. The hawk
was still hunting.
The sea came closer and kept making its sound.

Punch and the Judy

He feels so old, something primordial,
something that surfaced through the permafrost
sliding blindly towards warmth . . .
Icy against her back: she dreams herself
diving through breakers in a winter sea.

Rain at three and rain again at seven,
hanging leaden in the tidy square.
Dawn after dawn—detritus from the whirlpool,
the spars and splinters of shipwreck.
Walls of water roar beside the windows.

The girl's blonde head is drawn
into a caul of weed
and her long legs trawl the dark.
His shoulders rap the sea-bed. There comes
a noise like singing as their bodies sunder.

Picked over by dabbing fish.—
Her plump lips on his face and on his neck,
dampness of hair uncoiling.
His mind comes loose: he sees a figure
out on the drowning streets,

camouflaged by morning twilight,
watching the room, his eyes
luminous, like an assassin's.
Her shadow runs on the curtain, then she floats,
a tangle of pink and gold on frosted glass.

Love is his energy and his trap, spurring
the thug beneath the skin: homunculus
hooknosed, hunchbacked . . . Her voice
rings in the shower . . . It stirs in its cage of ribs,
inarticulate and murderous and mad.

Punch and the Passing Fancy

They had the same name
for each other.
They evolved
points of recognition.

Marking distances
that narrowed—
in the street, in the park—
they gained on themselves.

Always the first
to wake, she'd sip
his breathings-out,
crusty and toxic;

he would soak
in her dew:
a vagrant sleeper
in some drenched place.

They unearthed
mysteries of kinship,
something quick
in the blood,

witching, venereal;
their hermitage
echoed, each day,
to cooing and crowing.

They traded
only in bliss,
taking their haul
to cafés, to theatre queues.

By firelight
she told stories
of the antedeluvian
world of friendships—

here were the sole survivors,
passionate mutants
too fragile
to prosper or breed.

Punch in the Ancient World

Samos

Punch was horny
in the heat. His . . . thing
knocked his leg.

The beach-girls' bodies
were as functional as kitchenware.
They ran up from the sea
naked, a film of warm water peeling
from each overcooked breast.

He could taste blood
at the back of his throat—
a hound
led out for the chase.

They drowsed in the sun
placid, unsmudged.

He wanted them to see
the prophet's head
singing among stones

and rapture advancing
on the edge of a blade.

Patmos

The teenage refugees
trekked between the Amex office
and the harbour bar, where Punch

performed at noon and dusk:
boozy burlesque; he'd empty the place
with his tales and his wide eyes.

A voice from a cloud, he said, from stones,
from the sea, from deep
in the hillside's clutter of caves.

Light everlasting (promised the voice)
the light of holy retribution, and a sword
to level sinners. He showed

one boy his girlfriend, spread
in a vineyard, slammed across
a rock, her back

broken by rabid passion; to the girl
he showed the body of the boy
on the goat-path near their tent

and the swarm of ants
at his opened throat. Old Punch in drink
tends to stop at nothing.

Next morning, he strode through the waves
up to his waist
and spread his fingers beneath the suds

of backwash; tiny fish
nibbled at the joints and fluttered
fan-like across the buckle on his belt.

You only have to look out
with the land behind you
to become touchless.

The sun
like a cauldron on his shoulder
signalled from mirrors in the sea.

He wanted to be drawn alive
into its dense, white heart; to be part
of the endless eruption

that women flock to
with their oils and their flesh,
to be changed.

Athens

'If nothing works',
he thumbed her lip,
'I could kill you to keep you.'

She half-heard that; the day
flooded with chances. Sunlight
drilled at the shutters.

She went to the window.
She touched herself
lightly, between the legs,

like someone alone.
Breakfast first
and then an expedition.

The streets were hotting up.
Each vendor's stall
wore a fringe of crucifixes.

'Can you hear?' His petitions
could be stacked, she thought,
and counted, like loose change.

Punch on the Boul' Mich

Girls in the Luxembourg Gardens, girls on the boulevard.
The appalling tyranny of unfoxed loveliness.

Punch relaxed with his anis. He conjured
a parade of vulvas, threshing moistly.

He picked her out by the way the air
enveloped her—a dog's recognition.

She mooched through the leaf-dapple. In her poured denim
and narrow boots, she was love's be-all.

Later, she almost fainted
on the precipice of Notre Dame. Punch saw

a body spread on the coping beneath the rose window,
still fashionable in death: the anglepoise wrists

and nerveless backward look
of shop-front dummies on the Rue du Bac.

The gargoyles clucked. They looked like relatives.
She swayed but hung on, swooning at verticals.

With a flick of his fingernail he stole a note
from Quasimodo's bell—old hunchback, brother,

innocent. The flow of the pitch
as it climbed made her eyes roll back.

In the hour *entre chien et loup* she came into her own.
Neon streaked her hair. The whores

turned from her line of approach, as scavengers
scent a predator. To amuse him, she walked ahead

canting her hip-bones to make her haunches roll
and he pictured her body's bedrock, the uterine siftings

a seepage between boulders. When she settled
at a table, he sauntered past

then backtracked to play the pickup, noting her face
as docile as a print on glass.

Punch and the White Madonna

She watched them torture each other
with money; her flawless eyes
detected loss before all else.
In the calms between curses and tears,
or during the torn-off kisses, she'd record it.

Spirit of the household,
she counted the drinks. One morning
there was blood on the floor by her shelf,
as if she had drawn it.

A face
perfectly set for enduring.
The cheekbone moulds
the cheek to glacial smoothness and her cowl
falls in haggard lines beside it.
Her lips have been scalded white
by his terrible rages.

Any thought of the flesh
dissolves before she can hold it.
She would overhear
the wrench of love-cries from a farther room
and read them as pain, but share
his dreams of the unmarked features of children.

She suffers the household accident.
A slip of the blade
will tender a sacrament.
He offered the bread, then ate
with the musty taste of water to seal it.

The faintest music
rolls in the brittle dome of her brow,
a whispering
gallery of woodwind sounds.
She would gather a note and hold it
so long that its passionate tremor
threatened to crack the marble, so long
that its constancy was a silence
like the silence that lodges between planets.

Sometimes he felt she might almost turn
to a tap at the window,
a clock-chime, or the sudden
sensation of shattered plates.
The movement lies
in her, but she can't perfect it.

Beneath the white headdress, her head
has the brow-band and chin-band to bind it.
The strapping confines her
as comfortably as a small illness.
Any gesture, any word,
would blemish her. She abides
in the mysteries of quietness, the quiet
gaze, the quiet, cruel
passivity women are born to.

If he drinks himself to sleep, she mulls
the patter of his dream-talk
while he flounders on the couch.
She wonders at it,
but neither flinches nor smiles; she mounts guard
on her convert as the night-long, soft
wham of the river-wind plucks at his eyelids
and rainwater rams
its endless meekness underneath the door.

Punch's Gallery

Rouault: A Portrait

Outside by the sculpture garden, she tries to doze
in New York's grimy sun. To ease
the pain between her hips, she drags her knees
onto the iron bench, letting the breeze
lift her skirt. Perhaps she's guessed his ruse
is to watch from the window and feels his eyes
nudging her as he looks out, through a maze
of sundered spectra like a fool's disguise,
at her features clubbed with shadow. Booze
loosens them later; when he starts to seize
some advantage with blind craving, she goes
over to fill his glass. He shies,
but lets her pour. The whisky plays
rising notes in the bottleneck. A graze
from the metal slats she posed on, draws
his hand. The illness wells and flows,
bringing a fever with it, as she grows
whorish, eccentric, quick to please.

Giacometti: Woman With Her Throat Cut

A rictus. He wants to climb on top
and tongue the bronze
for its small electric shock. The limbs are flung
down like tree trunks lopped
and stripped—left in a place
the noise has moved on from and the dust
has settled in. Whatever joys
assembled her body to grace
congeal to black blood in the joints;
a raw last syllable
has cracked in her underjaw:
the end of blessings and taunts.

A noise outside the room
turns him. Her past lovers shuffle in
and gather silently. Their faces burn
with innocence. Each of them, groomed
for mourning, brings some keepsake.
The same few bars
of Haydn, like a recollected name,
badger them as they take
position where she's slammed against the wall.
The mole like a witch's mark,
the thatch thinning to trail
along her inner thigh—a faint cross-hatch . . .
But they'd know her in the dark
from the way her hands would shift
their hands. One by one they leave
for better things. He stands
alone with his feeble gift.

Some distant figures in the city square
know she is there, but cannot break
their silence to advise, although the air
between them is tense
with what remains of what they fear to speak.
A lean dog cranes
from its armature of ribs to guzzle her scents.

Schiele: *Standing Self-Portrait*

In stark sorrow he straddled his hand,
torso dim in the full-length glass,
the yellow night-light
staining his arm and naked haunch.

From knees to neck
a bundle of stumpy joints like truncheons;
an amputee
wizened by week-long fasts in the littered room.

He could see a coxcomb of spiky hair,
blotches of stubble,
the black naevus of bed-dirt
tracing his laugh-lines.

He gave tongue at the pleasure
and answered himself and fell against his face,
breath lightening the hair's breadth of darkness.
The image trembled

like a stirring in water just below the surface.
A pale torpedo
nudged the underside, the rind of silver,
then sank, a dying fish in mercury.

His fever flailed him:
starvation, lust, the torpor of the damned.
He went back to bed
and lay so the rails of his ribs

looped like the unstitched lath of a Viking longship;
figurehead, spars, the rest unholy wreckage.
He watched the weather in the garden, the black
taffeta of trees and dripping ivies.

27

The world described a long ellipse—
from his temples, past the straits of the bed,
closing at the high brick wall
and the plane-tree, just out of focus.

Unmoving, as if he were bandaged and hooked to pulleys . . .
Something back from his eyes
fused and guttered. His skin
flaked. His muscles jumped and snagged.

Hours and days . . . His mouth
grew mossy and sour as an old well.
He felt his capillaries puckering, his body salts
sifting and caking above the blood's tideline.

Ensor: Masks Confronting Death

A widow, her womb
shrunk to a walnut, hefts
her skirts, frolicking, wagging her hips
to seduce. She's rouged
like a whore. Will she put
some marrow back in those bones?

A girl in the flush of power,
impeccable, everything
watchable, lets her hand
be pressed to the naked teeth. She knows
she's not going home
with him tonight.

A murderer, the victim
still on his tongue,
looks at the eyes that look
through the girl's disguise. There follows
a brief, triangular
recognition. She shakes her head.

Punch, in the crowd with his stick,
is rabble-rousing,
as ever. His claque are baying; their sharp
snouts mark them out,
their whisky smell. He whacks
legs and grins invisibly.

Bonnard: Breakfast

1

An eyelid flickers, startled by the glass,
then droops in anticipation of the brush.

She starts on an indrawn breath. Her mouth goes slack.
Touch by touch she thickens every lash.

2

She does it naked. When she stoops to be
nose to nose with herself, her breasts make globes

clean of the rib-cage. There are poles of light
in the coppice beyond the lawn. A ground-mist ebbs.

3

Ovals and angles: he pictures the slope of her shoulder,
a hoisted hip, and lets a minute lapse

between placing their plates and knives and going to fetch
the basket of bread. A rhombus; a dark ellipse.

4

Water boils for the eggs. Chasing a thought
he sees it turn to confront him. *There's a smell* . . .

She is choosing a dress. He guesses she'll put it back
then choose another and put that back as well.

5

She might decide to stroll (he draws the bolt
on the tall french windows) shoeless across the grass

and then by the terrace, the stones holding her spoor.
She would see the table he's set: his place, her place.

6

She never looks in a mirror to brush her hair,
so she opens the blinds to view the day, hanging

her head to left and right for the volley of strokes.
The garden rocks on a pivot. Her ears are ringing.

7

It is whisky, the sourness rising in his nose
and scorching the membrane. His eye traces a smudge

above the skirting-board . . . She has come to the stair . . .
An ounce of glass litters the window-ledge.

8

He has posed her there, but can't make her descend,
or smile, or speak. He wonders, was it rash

to have picked that dress, to have left her feet unshod?
The welt on her cheek comes and goes like a blush.

Punch and the Gulls

1

One screamed from a chimney-pot, neck ducked,
spine taut, like a woman being fucked.

Punch howled and flapped his arms. She wouldn't fly.
Her world lapsed at the limit of her cry.

2

One harried a carcass on the beach,
hopped to and fro on tidemarked legs to reach

the riven torso, tore the flobby lung
and clapped the blood-clots underneath her tongue.

3

He watched another, frame by frame, displace
the arrested movements of a form in space.

She turned in the thermal, unperturbed, unjust,
lusted after, unimpeached by lust.

Punch as Victim

When she undressed, thoughtlessly, ready for bed,
taking her blouse off last, as always, her arse

a white pout topping the suntanned legs, he'd be there
with his imbecile grin; the little pool

of silk on the bedroom floor was his
to clean up. He'd pick hairs out of the bath

or open her bottles of cream when she wasn't there,
sniffing the surfaces, putting a dab

on the flaky skin above his jaw. One night
she bamboozled him with flattery; he slumped

onto the brace of her back in time to feel
the hiss of displeasure, a fleeting vibrato, fading

along the ripple of backbone. Her head stayed up;
she was looking straight at the wall, while he dropped

his cheek on her shoulder and stared at the bridge
her hand made on the sheet. The rings she wore

trickled light from stone to stone. The mash of his breath
was acrid, even to him. He unplugged and sat

back on his haunches as she subsided
and stayed there until she slept. Sometimes, he'd take

their photograph albums into his room and croon
with anticipation from moment to moment. The one

he liked best was a foggy shot—she was wearing his jacket
and scarf; if he half-closed his eyes

he could see himself, his fists dug into the pockets, the sly
courting of the camera, the moping lip. That day

the sun burned in the puddles. 'Remember', he'd ask,
'the story I told on the phone?' She remembered it all

and watched him upend the decanter. His sleight of hand
was lifting terrible images from a glance

to left or right, from an absence, from some coy
pose as she window-shopped. His memories

ran with him like a dog-pack. The glorious prospect of sin
and discovery kept him alert. He'd lie

close as a poacher to catch her
at the sink, side-lit, applying a *gant de toilette*,

knees splayed like a dancer's, her features set
in vacuity, seamless, unransomed by hope or regret.

Punch as Patient

The pain was endless, endless; then it stopped
and that was much more sinister. He knew
it was gathered in some nerveless place, holed up.

Outside was another country: the slow gulls
settling on dead-straight furrows, trees
motionless under frost. The bitter smell

it shed crept in the skylights. Someone coughed,
seeming to start a bustle in the ward.
They were bringing trays and trolleys. Someone passed

behind a curtain by a side-ward, moving
across the place where light was shed each night
from beneath a green lampshade. He recognised

her manner of showing impatience, the flap
of a hand and swinging hair.
The mirage moved the curtain. Her postcard lay

on the bedside table, between the barley-water
with its patina of dust and the noxious antirrhinums.
His mind's eye focused on the lines: the way

she'd use a capital mid-word. 'By heart,'
he thought, 'I have her, now, by heart.'
When they came, in the lamplit evening, with the pill

that blacked him out, he'd say
some formless, shame-faced prayers: to live
always in passion, to die in the moment that she died.

The pain snicked out and touched him, like
a dirty needle. He yelped and ground his eyes shut.
Colours ran, like acid, from the cornea,

etching the dark shape of her head lifted
to question, becoming her silhouette, advancing,
arms akimbo in astonishment.

Punch the Anchorite

The gale stoppered his mouth
(for once) and gave him cover.
He watched the grass seethe

in close-up against the horizon,
smelled the mud, heard the cypress
hiss its kyrie eleison

as he lay wrapped in his chains,
straitened by love.
A past poured out like grains

of salt, too sharp to taste,
spice without food . . .
Her glorious, phony Christ

of mad extremes, his own
affliction of words, the falls
from grace, the lean

years, his sickness and sin.
He put his face to the wall:
the buttress: his pen;

he'd hammered himself to the boss
where the surface sweated
sweet water, an abacus on moss

hung now with the world's new image,
tors and declivities. An eye
opened. The intricate tonnage

stirred, its shadows broke
in the wet light. A fever
had been weathered. He woke

in the blood-warmth of home,
sipped from the clavicle, licked
minerals from her armpit's dome.

Punch's Nightmares 1

They entered the house. The other man
was familiar—his accent, his shipboard walk—
but his name was tuneless and garbled.

They were there for some purpose: the steel cache
of rods and ratchets chimed
as he set the toolbag down on the flagstones.

The place seemed deserted. They went from door to door.
Crystal drops on the chandeliers filtered the sunlight
to chips of rainbow against the walnut panels. It was

a dog they could hear, whimpering somewhere
further back than they wanted to go. Portraits lined
the staircase; their palms squeaked

as they stroked the polished ballustrades. She lay
on the bathroom floor. Her throat was slashed
and wrenched, so the crown of her head

and her heels bore the weight
of the rigid arc of her body. He gathered her up
as if touching were healing. She spoke;

through the purple and pork-fat-white of the gash
she whispered, 'He's still
in the house. He's still in the house.'

The other man left to look. She turned in the arms
that held her, like someone settling to sleep,
pliable, and she sighed, taking his warmth.

He woke in the dark and scribbled her name
on the bedside writing-pad, then settled to sleep.
They entered the house. They went from door to door.

Punch's Nightmares 2

He was a mouth on a pole
shouting orders from the dug-out.
The mud looked like melted coffee ice-cream.

When the noise stopped
he thought about getting back
to wherever he'd been when he left her.

The officers were dead.
If she'd really known them all, then why,
he wondered, wasn't she here

to keen over the rumpled gas-bags of bodies?
He stood in a nest of sinew
soppy with blood

and sniffed the air.
A pace or so from the trench, she stopped
and watched the poison billow in the craters,

hearing him say, again, that he'd never desert.
He framed the distinguished face
between two ruptured tree trunks, just in case

he'd have to remember her like that.
'You're okay,' she said. 'What a place!' A cadaver
stirred in the mire.

Punch's Nightmares 3

First it was a railway station. He admired
the frogging on his father's uniform, noted the way
the old man tapped the fringe of his moustache

with the topside of a finger when they'd kissed.
The train pulled out. He was surprised
to find himself the passenger.

A dark-room next.
He stood behind the hands of the technician
and watched the damson-coloured mark

grow on her back like a flaw in the paper.
The photograph turned sepia; a text
and caption fixed the place and used his name.

Then a fashionable street. The mannequins,
with perfect nipples and nails,
fixed blind eyes on the spotlights . . .

Behind plate-glass, surrounded
by the soft hues of the season, Punch
poured tea for the Femmes de Venise.

His father stopped to peer in, cracking
a boot with his swagger-stick. The women
swivelled their heads like birds.

She offered a scone and jam. The livid pulp
of burn-scars, the tunnel-nostrils, gleamed
like tin-foil. He took the food and ate.

Punch's Nightmares 4

She sloughed the old skin off.
The new skin glistened, transparent:
a smell of paraffin.

Between the purple coils
and bulbous tucks of entrail
he could see his children, backed up

in her womb. She lay
on the dampened sheet, gin-clear,
a weft of muscle

pursing to make a frill
that ran on her belly, like
an undersea current.

The mesh of hair in her groin,
the blots of her nipples,
were delicate abstracts. She'd lost

years of soil: handclasps,
the courtesies of dancing partners,
hapless gestures, the tincture

flesh leaves on flesh.
The straps and ribbing of clothes
would have bruised her; perfume

would have smoked on her wrists and neck.
From the pearl of her heel to the soft
fingernails, she was untouched.

He dreamt he was dreaming all this
and waited to wake
from his own weightless tread,

from the blue stage-glow
that lit the dream, from sound
suspended, until he saw

her lips, bonded
like blown glass, incorruptible, and her eyes
white with ecstasy.

Punch's Nightmares 5

A dark blue evening after snowfall,
the air so still that a human cry
or the slur of a starter-motor
could be heard from hilltop to hilltop,

the crust of snow unbroken for miles,
the freeze deepening. They'd retreated
as far as they could go—
Punch and the child and the nurse;

the attic's porthole windows were crowded
with pine-tree tops, the small boughs loosing
volleys of snow, then whipping
back into silence. Old Foxface:

the rub and shuffle on the stair
beyond the barricaded door. The child
looked up from the caul of the nurse's arms
towards the sound outside; his wound

was edged with a dark rind, and deep,
a wedge cut from a pomegranate.
Its bruised marblings sweated
beads of blood, like dew, making

a shadow of damp on the dressing.
Trains crossed the viaduct beyond
the pheasant-wood each hour
like hamlets on the move; evacuees

hugged their bundles in sleep. Punch rooted
among the lumber, in search
of a signal-light or a weapon. Sidetracked
by the family albums, he dreamed

of hooves rapping the stones
in the stable yard as he leaned
to take the stirrup-cup; a girl,
veiled and gloved and plundering the hives.

A draught from the door brought in
the stench of saltpetre, a scorch
that cracked his sinuses, but he kept the book
in front of his face.

'I'll never live there again.'—
He spoke it aloud. 'I could give him my breast—
just for comfort,' she whispered,

'I can't think of anything else.' The child
whimpered and sat up suddenly.
'Please,' he said, 'there's something
coming out of my bandage.'

Punch's Nightmares 6

He rooted round in the trench.
It had living-space.
Dream-logic made it a tiny room
without books; there was
a skylight no one had cleaned for months.

He trotted home. She was brewing morning tea
and walked through him
to go to the fridge for milk.
She was humming *Banks and Braes*.
His hands were smoke on her throat.

Pace for pace, in step,
he walked her up the tree-lined avenue
to the butcher's. She bought
pate and cold roast beef—enough
for two. He screamed in her face

and she butted his mouth
while sauntering to the door.
They passed the day
in galleries (nothing to like),
a cafe, a shoe-shop, the garden . . .

His herbs were still growing
and the firethorn had recovered. At dusk
she poured her first drink; ice
cracked in the glass;
he could taste what her lip touched.

They answered the door.
They hurried from stove to table.
He sat in the empty chair.
The conversation boomed
in his rib-cage like whispers in cloisters.

He staked-out the bedroom
and waited an hour for her cries, her knees
jacked up, the wet smell.
She enjoyed and enjoyed and enjoyed. Punch gibbered;
he stood alongside and howled;

he put a fist in her mouth and tugged
at her teeth; he settled
on her like ash; exhausted, he crawled
to the foot of the bed, like a dog,
to wait for the clock to wake her.

Punch's Nightmares 7

The blind backs of houses
formed endless alleys, smooth
and pitted as ancient leather.
There were soldiers and flares.
He loped past with his hound.

She entered to applause,
courting the footlights, following
a cart. She was sifting
the faces of the near-dead.

He walked in the wheel-ruts
to where they'd stopped for the night.
He peered over
the stable door. The driver
was at her like a boar.

Next morning she rode
on the tailgate, trailing her legs.
The bodies clattered like laths.
He saw them off
into the wings. She'd never
find him among the stiffs.

Now he came centre-stage.
Now his soliloquy,
his grace-note, the moment of moments
when he'd gloss the conceit.
The packed house hung
on his indrawn breath. Backstage
the soldiers ran
from door to door with their torches.

The Blessed Punchinello, Mart.

He would live in unapproachable light
and the numbing silence of denial,
weathered in desert air
to leather and bone, a shrivelled sun dial

welded by bone to the pillar: and record
rumours of the world
as a feather on a stripped nerve.
His hands, both curled

like tubers in his lap,
would cease to learn
the wintry rituals of supplication.
Every day, his lean

shadow would run to lodge its tip
like a splinter beneath her skin.
He'd grow remote
and unignorable, the thin

end of a wedge, a silenced voice
listened for like the plummet of an echo
when the land-line shrinks,
when the city starts to glow

raising a false dawn and the hum
of vast machines
puckers the skin on the river.
He would know what reduction means,

the beauty of anorexia, the slow
smelting of martyrs! A fever
would scorch his eyes, the noon sky
flare with visions, then shrink to the shiver

and rustle of gnats at evening.
The scratch of his stubble growing, the least
tremor on the air, would touch his senses:
the lightest breath of the beast

splashing the plinth below
then trotting towards the suburbs, her spoor
hot in its nostrils, a dream of extravagance
swamping the pink-black mottle of its jaw.

Mr Punch Confronts his God

The stonework soared,
but inch by bloodstained inch. His shout
churned in a vacuum of arches and rafters.

A pain welled in his shoulder and ran
the length of the bones in his arm;
he flexed his fist to let it find a level;

it sank to a low ache,
tugging his thumb in a spasm that matched
his heartbeat. He felt

as if he'd been tranced. His voice
and the sharp flow in his arm
seemed an awakening.

Deep in the swimming particles of dusk
the dying figure
throbbed on the cross. Who could survive

that ardour? Not popes, not kings,
not Cuthbert on his rock
flayed by the northern winds,

pinned there by troth, perceiving
an awesome response in the ocean rising
and running bleak green on the stone . . .

A wind lifted the spray: a distant whisper
no louder than bridehood closing
its petals to seal a canker; then

all fear, all morbid love, all words
to celebrate, all paint to thumb the eye
all music's power to stun,

rose in his mind, gathered, and was lost:
a knowledge he'd never owned
nor sought. A light came on

in the porch, so he walked to the door,
his heeltaps ringing like asdic in the flags.
A glow from the rich glass patched

the dark facade. In every cleft
angels clung, or swarmed on the wall like bats.
Some sulphurous eye was watching as he left.

Punch at his Devotions

A dab of water
sizzles on his forehead.
His knee cracks
acknowledging the Presence.
Punch has a weakness
la-la
    for this Lady.

*   *   *

'Virgin, intercede. I have lusted
for those of your sex
till my bones ached.
Chirrup-chirrup
        I bit
the silky backs of their necks
and they whimpered with glee.'

*   *   *

'Another sin: I squandered
happiness, wanting ecstasy.
You understand.
Those ragged faces
I pitchforked into passion
            la-la
coaching the mild in fury.'

*   *   *

'My Dear, My Dearest, Dear One,
do your best.
I have lied for advantage; I sulked
and they brought me themselves
in pretty dresses. I prayed
for someone's death
as you know . . .'

*   *   *

'Do you remember the church
of S. Niccolo dei Mendicoli?
What I spoke of then
won't resolve in prayer.
Light flared
on windows above the lagoon
and the city went dead. You wore
your customary blue gown.'

*   *   *

'I held myself in contempt; Lady,
I flogged myself with inventions.
Chirrup
         such indulgences!
Everything tends to disruption. Yesterday
there were silhouettes
cut on the curtain: whoever
inhabits the garden. Their features
were grey
and warped by the ruche.'

*   *   *

'Of your charity
            la-la
                    I conjured
angels for amusement. Intercede.
They performed their pinpoint dance
with sad smiles.
In the dark, it seemed
their wings clapped my back
and the fever shrank.'

                *   *   *

'Loved One, Flawless Mirror,
Tamer of Unicorns, Dove,
Star of the Sea, I enter
a plea of diminished laughter.
I've fasted. I've kept vigil
with whiskies past dawn,
for Christ's sake. It's enough.
Why does there seem to be,
outside those odd rooms
with loaded dressing-tables,
always the drone of engines?'

                *   *   *

The Body of Christ. Amen.
                            'Please intercede.
Have a word. Do what you can
la-la
        Lady, negotiate.

I fled and he followed me, flying.

Chirrup-chirrup
                la-la, la-la
la
    Lamb of God.'

Punch at Peace with Himself

The particles slowed
all in harmony. The weft
of hair on his forearm gleamed
like wheat turned by a wind.

His apeish thoughts went
out of focus
then ran together, a soup
of tints and tones.

He hummed one note:
a dynamo, shutting down.
He lay in lines. His limp
dick was a damp squib.

His lungs puckered, just.
The piebald, waxy rill
on his jawline and throat
was fats and fluids setting.

Things gathered to leave.
The garden was shut in
by rain; he stared
at the water-lights and grinned

a baby's grin. Keeping discreet
station behind his eye-line
(her skirts rustled) sat
the beloved executrix.

Punch's Day Book

'They've stacked your pictures in among the books.
There are flowers and cushions, but nobody goes in
to work or read. The house
is full of music always.
                              Will you become
a monk, with your manuscripts
and your winnowing, skin-deep lust?
Will you never
recover from your life? At every turn
there is something
to tear you, or make you afraid.'

'Almost nothing moves
in your universe of phantoms. Nothing revives.
A lifetime's words have puddled in you, like gall.
Not fury, but the residue of fury.
Not love, but love's cold junk of bones.
                                        Pretend
the window has been flung back; you are standing
close to the downpour. Everything floods with green.
There's no beginning
and no end to the moment.'

'Mornings are worse. Do you
find that? I wake as light arrives
at every crevice in the house. The birds
are a chorus of women
thrilled by new possessions. I might hear
the church bell, an aeroplane
descending in steps . . . The world
is close, but outside:
beyond the window-sill, beyond the gate,
a guileless cryptogram.

I shall die of my thoughts. I've become
my story's heroine
saturated by disease, the last
of the beautiful tuberculars.

All this would be solved
if I had you between the pulses of my wrists.'

'When you pray, what do you want?
I ask the almost-possible.
My days are carried on the backs of birds.
I can feel a purpose about me, undefined,
some mornings, on waking . . . some mornings, not.
It is folly to doze till noon and folly not to.
I lie in a pouch of odours, planning risks
and the world saunters past. Last week
I dreamt we were young, the children were young,
it was autumn, an evening, heat still lay
in the walls of our house,
the children slept on our laps,
damp, white curls, the tiny stitching of breath,
and we cradled our first drinks of the day . . . Of course,
I dreamt no such thing, not I.
The dogs go everywhere with me now.
I return from my morning ride
business-like with parings of hoof and horn
for the compost's mulch. I'm a Victorian lady
working my garden, wearing
broderie-anglaise and my white straw hat,
leaving slipper marks in the dew.
If you could see me
wandering here! I pause
on the bridge over the stream, or settle
with book and glass
beneath the pear tree's quaint strappado.'

The hang of her brow
over a book, her wrists
crossed one on the other below the page,
or the vent of an eye
as she looked away, revealed
the bloodline of Saxonish neurotics.

There was low music, slow,
caught in the roll of woodsmoke
blotting the summer garden.
Something made her look away,
sharply, towards the stream
and the circle of chairs beside the orchard.

One moment reading, wrists loosely crossed,
the next, head lifted, alert,
the pose of a creature
disturbed at its feeding: a fixed
stare; then, reassured, she dropped her gaze
to the page, half-hearing the music perhaps.

You could see the blush of health
beneath the furze on her cheek,
the brightness of the creature's eye.

'That summer, our youth astounded me.
The house still fixes my dreams; I read
or walk by the stream, past the orchard.

You were edgy, or so it seemed;
eager to be away.
Then, as now, your words impoverished me.'

'I hoard my luck: a brooch, a knot of straw. I try
to marry the tune to the rhyme. Sometimes
I move things from here to there—
a housewife's coup d'etat.
                                    The skipping-song
had a beat like a muffled drum. You brought
food on a tray. The children released
their starry, gluttonous smiles into my care.

The writing-desk shall be so,
this chair might stand
beside the hearth, the pictures shall be so,
and each room have its bowl of pot-pourri.'

'I turn the page. Smoke streams in my lungs
leaving them damp and stretched. All human shock
gathers in the chill of three a.m. Across the county
shutters are closed against the wind. Some menace,
lean with spite, comes with the early silence
as if wolves still ran the hillsides, quartering
an old killing ground, the skyline shrunk
to cameo inside a yellow iris.'

'My lover has foxy teeth and keeps two dogs.
Perhaps you remember him.
He'll hoist me over a cask and lift my skirt
at any time.
              It all goes well,
you can see I'm feeling well.
The dogs hunt every spinney if I slip them
and come back flecked with blood.

They said the weather would break.
                                    I won't have children
whatever tricks he tries. To be outlived
is terrifying.
              At times
the summer seemed to have lasted half the year.
Really, I came to think
I could be here forever, the valley's stoic
gathering small virtues, a student of leaf and fruit.
The ascetic wants to shine in the eye of God.'

'I try to progress my life minute by minute.
The striking clocks have been sold, so I cannot tell
how long it takes you
to do the things I invent for you to do.
The people I give you to meet
are witty and anchored to circumstance.

I shall make a nursery rhyme
about the creature in this Christmas photograph:
mop-haired, the scourge of children.
My dreams deliver confidences.
I am ransacked, I am open to the weather,
I echo with pleasantries.

My next task is to sort
the dead images into piles—with good grace.
When you read this, picture me
serene beneath my sheet,
at my foot, the cocktail-shaker; at my head
a table of oils, guaranteeing preservation.'

'There are those who plan to die
blameless, open-handed, an unwritten letter.
We can't aspire to that.
We lack the pure compulsion and the nerve.

The orchard's harvested; the stoves are lit
to burn all winter; the house is steeped
in a musty odour of fruit.
                    Think how it is
to own nothing, to carry nothing
from one place to the next . . .
Unburdened, my body grows
featureless. I could disappear in water,
be perfectly matched to grassland.
                    Every tree
is stripped and life goes on underground;
even the telephone's in hibernation.

I shall be here, of course,
seeing the season out from my fireside chair,
sometimes bringing apples down from the loft
or walking to church. If I should stray,
how would you ever find me?—
a pallid silhouette
on a clear road, like any refugee.'

'A night-long blow, seeded with sleet
as if a door had been opened on the north . . .

I am mobbed by shadows.
The future is codified

a serial-number die-stamped on my bones.'

'The Devon love-knot
the gleaming bevel
of the ha-ha, the beeches, the pic of you
emerging with a tray, ha-ha

the pic, the snap
the children dancing
your finger fingering my quim, ha-ha
ha-ha, the knot, the bright bevel

ha-ha'